THIS JOURNAL BELONGS TO

_____

DATE

_____

Let love and faithfulness never leave you;
bind them around your neck,
write them on the tablet of your heart.
Then you will win favor and a good name in
the sight of God and man.
Trust in the LORD with all your heart
and lean not on your own understanding;
in all your ways submit to him,
and he will make your paths straight.

PROVERBS 3:3-6 NIV

YOU ARE A BELOVED CHILD OF GOD, PRECIOUS TO HIM IN EVERY WAY.
As you seek Him, He will show you the mysteries of life and unfold
His unique plans for you—a life full of rich blessing and wisdom.
God cares about you and knows all the desires of your heart.
He is as close as breathing.

Let this journal inspire you to express your thoughts,
record your prayers, embrace your dreams, and listen
to what God is saying to you through the book of Proverbs.
Trust in the Lord and let His Word be written on your heart.

Those who are steadily learning how to love are enabled to do this because the very love of God, Himself, has been put into our hearts.

EUGENIA PRICE

Do not let wisdom and understanding out of your sight,
preserve sound judgment and discretion; they will be life for you,
an ornament to grace your neck.

PROVERBS 3:21–22 NIV

Wise is the person who can take the little moment as it comes
and make it brighter before it's gone.

The way of the righteous is like the first gleam of dawn,
which shines ever brighter until the full light of day.

PROVERBS 4:18 NLT

Sometimes it is necessary for us to speak. At other times it is important
that we be quiet. Wisdom comes with knowing the difference.

MRS. D. E. CLAY

Gold there is, and rubies in abundance,
but lips that speak knowledge are a rare jewel.

PROVERBS 20:15 NIV

Friends are an indispensable part of a meaningful life. They are the ones who share our burdens and multiply our blessings. A true friend sticks by us in our joys and sorrows. In good times and bad, we need friends who will pray for us, listen to us, and lend a comforting hand and an understanding ear when needed.

BEVERLY LaHAYE

There are "friends" who destroy each other,
but a real friend sticks closer than a brother.

PROVERBS 18:24 NLT

You can never change the past. But by the grace of God, you can win the future. So remember those things which will help you forward, but forget those things which will only hold you back.

RICHARD C. WOODSOME

The teaching of the wise is a fountain of life,
that one may turn away from the snares of death.

PROVERBS 13:14 ESV

If you desire to be really happy, you must
make God your final and ultimate goal.

THOMAS À KEMPIS

My children, listen to me,
for all who follow my ways are joyful.

PROVERBS 8:32 NLT

When we are told that God, who is our dwelling place, is also our fortress, it can only mean one thing, and that is that if we will but live in our dwelling place, we shall be perfectly safe and secure from every assault of every possible enemy that can attack us.

HANNAH WHITALL SMITH

Have no fear of sudden disaster or of the ruin that overtakes the wicked,
for the LORD will be at your side and will keep your foot from being snared.

PROVERBS 3:25–26 NIV

A true friend...advises justly, assists readily, adventures boldly, takes all patiently, defends courageously, and continues a friend unchangeably.

WILLIAM PENN

A word fitly spoken is like apples of gold in settings of silver.
Like an earring of gold and an ornament of fine gold
is a wise rebuker to an obedient ear.

PROVERBS 25:11–12 NKJV

Many receive advice; only the wise profit from it.

PUBLILIUS SYRUS

Without wise leadership, a nation falls;
there is safety in having many advisers.

PROVERBS 11:14 NLT

Wise people, even though all laws were abolished,
would still lead the same life.

ARISTOPHANES

I, wisdom, dwell together with prudence; I possess knowledge and discretion.
To fear the Lord is to hate evil; I hate pride and arrogance,
evil behavior and perverse speech. Counsel and sound judgment are mine;
I have insight, I have power.

PROVERBS 8:12–14 NIV

There is joy in heaven when a tear of sorrow is shed in the presence of a truly understanding heart. And heaven will never forget that joy.

CHARLES MALIK

The prospect of the righteous is joy,
but the hopes of the wicked come to nothing.

PROVERBS 10:28 NIV

The truth [is] that there is only one terminal dignity—love. And the story of a love is not important—what is important is that one is capable of love. It is perhaps the only glimpse we are permitted of eternity.

HELEN HAYES

Love prospers when a fault is forgiven,
but dwelling on it separates close friends.

PROVERBS 17:9 NLT

I account that one of the greatest demonstrations of real friendship, that a friend can really endeavor to have his friend advanced in honor, in reputation, in the opinion of wit or learning, before himself.

JEREMY TAYLOR

A friend loves at all times.

What a blessing is a friend with a heart so trustworthy that you may safely bury all your secrets in it, whose conscience you may fear less than your own, who can relieve your cares by his words, your doubts by his advice, your sadness by his good humor, and whose very look gives comfort to you.

Perfume and incense bring joy to the heart,
and the pleasantness of a friend springs from their heartfelt advice.

PROVERBS 27:9 NIV

If you have a habit of being attentive and expressing interest,
your children will not confuse your loving instruction with rejection.

CHARLES STANLEY

A fool despises his father's instruction,
but he who receives correction is prudent.
In the house of the righteous there is much treasure.

Advice is like snow: the softer it falls the longer it dwells upon,
and the deeper it sinks into the mind.

SAMUEL TAYLOR COLERIDGE

Plans succeed through good counsel;
don't go to war without wise advice.

All that is required to build a stable relationship is the desire to do so...
with a little advice and counsel. Ultimately, of course, we will rely
on the principles endorsed by the creator of families Himself.
That is pretty safe counsel.

JAMES DOBSON

Everyone enjoys a fitting reply; it is wonderful
to say the right thing at the right time!

PROVERBS 15:23 NLT

As we enter more and more deeply into this experience of being humbled and exalted, our knowledge of God increases, and with it our peace, our strength, and our joy. God help us, then, to put our knowledge about God to this use, that we all may in truth "know the Lord."

J. I. PACKER

Wisdom's instruction is to fear the LORD,
and humility comes before honor.

PROVERBS 15:33 NIV

Teach me, O Lord, to do Your will; teach me to live worthily
and humbly in Your sight; for You are my Wisdom.

THOMAS À KEMPIS

Commit your work to the LORD,
and your plans will be established.

PROVERBS 16:3 ESV

There is much satisfaction in work well done;
praise is sweet, but there can be no happiness equal
to the joy of finding a heart that understands.

VICTOR ROBINSON

Wise words bring many benefits,
and hard work brings rewards.

PROVERBS 12:14 NLT

A wise gardener plants his seeds, then has the good sense
not to dig them up every few days to see if a crop is on the way.
Likewise, we must be patient as God brings the answers...in His own good time.

QUIN SHERRER

Discretion is a life-giving fountain to those who possess it.

PROVERBS 16:22 NLT

The needed change within us is God's work, not ours. The demand
is for an inside job, and only God can work from the inside. We cannot attain
or earn this righteousness of the kingdom of God: it is a grace that is given.

RICHARD J. FOSTER

The one who sows righteousness reaps a sure reward....
Those who are righteous will go free.

PROVERBS 11:18, 21 NIV

A word of encouragement to those we meet, a cheerful smile in the supermarket, a card or letter to a friend, a readiness to witness when opportunity is given— all are practical ways in which we may let His light shine through us.

ELIZABETH B. JONES

A cheerful look brings joy to the heart;
good news makes for good health.

It is never enough to know about spiritual things with your mind.
Mental knowledge is not the same thing as truly understanding from the center
of your being, which results from experiencing and doing.

TERESA OF AVILA

Joyful is the person who finds wisdom, the one who gains understanding.
For wisdom is more profitable than silver, and her wages are better than gold.

PROVERBS 3:13–14 NLT

Make no little plans; they have no magic to stir one's blood and probably themselves will not be realized. Make big plans; aim high in hope and work, remembering that a noble, logical diagram once recorded will not die.

DANIEL H. BURNHAM

We can make our plans, but the LORD determines our steps.

God's wisdom is always available to help us choose from alternatives we face,
and help us to follow His eternal plan for us.

GLORIA GAITHER

The LORD directs our steps, so why
try to understand everything along the way?

PROVERBS 20:24 NLT

Courage is what it takes to stand up and speak;
courage is also what it takes to sit down and listen.

WINSTON CHURCHILL

Speak up for those who cannot speak for themselves,
for the rights of all who are destitute.

PROVERBS 31:8 NIV

The firmest friendships have been formed in mutual adversity;
as iron is most strongly united by the fiercest flame.

COLTON

As iron sharpens iron, so a friend sharpens a friend.

PROVERBS 27:17 NLT

You can learn to overcome the worry of anticipation. After you begin to experience more and more the ready success of divine grace upon all occasions, you will not worry about things before they happen. When the time comes for you to do your duty, you will find God as in a clear mirror, and He will empower you and make you fit to fulfill your obligations.

BROTHER LAWRENCE

Anxiety weighs down the heart,
but a kind word cheers it up.

PROVERBS 12:25 NIV

We shall steer safely through every storm, so long as our heart is right,
our intention fervent, our courage steadfast, and our trust fixed on God.

FRANCIS DE SALES

Whoever listens to me will dwell secure
and will be at ease, without dread of disaster.

PROVERBS 1:33 ESV

With God, life is eternal—both in quality and length. There is no joy comparable to the joy if discovering something new from God, about God. If the continuing life is a life of joy, we will go on discovering, learning.

EUGENIA PRICE

The fear of the LORD is a fountain of life,
turning a person from the snares of death.

PROVERBS 14:27 NIV

Communication is the meeting of meaning. When your meaning meets
my meaning across the bridge of words, tones, acts, and deeds,
when understanding occurs, then we know that we have communicated.

DAVID AUGSBURGER

Obey my commands and live! Guard my instructions as you
guard your own eyes. Tie them on your fingers as a reminder.
Write them deep within your heart. Love wisdom like a sister;
make insight a beloved member of your family.

PROVERBS 7:2–4 NLT

A conflict cannot be entered with the idea that one must "win."
There is no winning in a good conflict,
but a breaking through to better understanding of each other.

CAROLE MAYHALL

Good understanding gains favor,
but the way of the unfaithful is hard.

PROVERBS 13:15 NKJV

Wisdom often times consists of knowing what to do next.

HERBERT HOOVER

The one who gets wisdom loves life; the one
who cherishes understanding will soon prosper.

PROVERBS 19:8 NIV

True friendship thrives through media
Of touch and sight and speech,
But often in the silent times
It most extends its reach.

CRAIG E. SATHOFF

The wise in heart are called discerning,
and gracious words promote instructions.

PROVERBS 16:21 NIV

If you can help anybody even a little, be glad;
up the steps of usefulness and kindness,
God will lead you on to happiness and friendship.

MALTBIE D. BABCOCK

Do not withhold good from those who deserve it
when it's in your power to help them.

PROVERBS 3:27 NLT

Encouragement is being a good listener, being positive, letting others
know you accept them for who they are. It is offering hope,
caring about the feelings of another, understanding.

GIGI GRAHAM TCHIVIDJIAN

The fruit of the righteous is a tree of life,
and whoever captures souls is wise.

God is constantly taking knowledge of me in love,
and watching over me for my good.

J. I. PACKER

The LORD corrects those he loves, just as a father
corrects a child in whom he delights.

PROVERBS 3:12 NLT

May the God of love and peace set your heart at rest
and speed you on your journey.

RAYMOND OF PENYAFORT

In the fear of the Lord one has strong confidence,
and his children will have a refuge.

Personal perfection is impossible, but it is possible
to aim for genuineness, honesty, consistency, and moral purity,
and to frankly acknowledge it when we fail.

SUSAN ALEXANDER YATES

The way of the LORD is a stronghold to those with integrity,
but it destroys the wicked. The godly will never be disturbed, but the wicked will
be removed from the land. The mouth of the godly person gives wise advice....
The lips of the godly speak helpful words.

If God exists and we are made in His image we can have real meaning,
and we can have real knowledge through what He has communicated to us.

FRANCIS SCHAEFFER

Hold on to instruction, do not let it go;
guard it well, for it is your life.

PROVERBS 4:13 NIV

What keeps the Christian going...is the knowledge of God written on his or her heart.

LINDA CLARK

Apply your heart to instruction,
and your ears to words of knowledge.

PROVERBS 23:12 NKJV

God often calls us to do things that we do not have the ability to do.
Spiritual discernment is knowing if God calls you to do something,
God empowers you to do it.

SUZANNE FARNHAM

The wise in heart are called discerning,
and gracious words promote instruction.

PROVERBS 16:21 NIV

As light is pleasant to the eye,
so is truth to the understanding.

RICHARD PELHAM

The hearts of the wise make their mouths prudent,
and their lips promote instruction.

PROVERBS 16:23 NIV

Learning is not attained by change, it must be sought
for with ardor and attended to with diligence.

ABIGAIL ADAMS

The plans of the diligent lead surely to abundance,
but everyone who is hasty comes only to poverty.

Thank God every morning when you get up that you have something to do that day which must be done, whether you like it or not. Being forced to work, and forced to do your best, will breed in you temperance and self-control, diligence and strength of will, cheerfulness and contentment, and a hundred virtues which the idle never know.

CHARLES KINGSLEY

Lazy people don't even cook the game they catch,
but the diligent make use of everything they find.

PROVERBS 12:27 NLT

Concrete reasons for loving another human being not only need to be expressed to that person, but will also help the person who is doing the verbalizing. Dwelling in one's mind on logical reasons for love does not diminish the feelings of love, but increases them.

EDITH SCHAEFFER

A person's wisdom yields patience;
it is to one's glory to overlook an offense.

PROVERBS 19:11 NIV

How vital that we pray, armed with the knowledge that God is in heaven.
Pray with any lesser conviction and your prayers are timid, shallow, and hollow.
But spend some time walking in the workshop of the heavens, seeing what
God has done, and watch how your prayers are energized.

MAX LUCADO

A faithful person will be richly blessed.

PROVERBS 28:20 NIV

God's Word acts as a light for our paths. It can help scare off
unwanted thoughts in our minds and protect us from the enemy.

GARY SMALLEY AND JOHN TRENT

People with integrity walk safely, but those who follow crooked paths
will slip and fall. People who wink at wrong
cause trouble, but a bold reproof promotes peace.

PROVERBS 10:9-10 NLT

To acquire knowledge, one must study;
but to acquire wisdom, one must observe.

MARILYN VOS SAVANT

The heart of the discerning acquires knowledge;
the ears of the wise seek it out.

PROVERBS 18:15 NIV

A true friend is someone who listens to us with real concentration and expresses sincere care for our struggles and pains. She makes us feel that something very deep is happening to us.

SISTER HELEN FEENEY

An unreliable messenger stumbles into trouble,
but a reliable messenger brings healing.

All [God's] glory and beauty come from within, and there He delights to dwell.
His visits there are frequent, His conversation sweet, His comforts refreshing,
His peace passing all understanding.

THOMAS À KEMPIS

Buy the truth, and do not sell it,
also wisdom and instruction and understanding.

Knowledge is proud that it knows so much;
wisdom is humble that it knows no more.

WILLIAM COWPER

Wise people treasure knowledge,
but the babbling of a fool invites disaster.

PROVERBS 10:14 NLT

Justice and power must be brought together, so that whatever is just
may be powerful, and whatever is powerful may be just.

BLAISE PASCAL

I walk in the way of righteousness, along the paths of justice, bestowing
a rich inheritance on those who love me and making their treasuries full.

PROVERBS 8:20-21 NIV

I have learned from experience that the greater part of our happiness or misery depends on our dispositions and not on our circumstances.

MARTHA WASHINGTON

A merry heart does good, like medicine,
but a broken spirit dries the bones.

PROVERBS 17:22 NKJV

We were made for God. Only by being in some respect like Him, only by being a manifestation of His beauty, lovingkindness, wisdom, or goodness, has any earthly beloved excited our love.

C. S. LEWIS

Wisdom...will place a lovely wreath on your head;
she will present you with a beautiful crown.

PROVERBS 4:8-9 NLT

Reflection...enables our minds to be stretched in three different directions—
the direction that leads to a proper relationship with God, the relationship
that leads to a healthy relationship with others, and the relationship
that leads to a deeper understanding of oneself.

MARK CONNOLLY

A truly wise person uses few words; a person
with understanding is even-tempered.

PROVERBS 17:27 NLT

It might be a good idea to ask ourselves how we develop our capacity to choose for joy. Maybe we could spend a moment at the end of each day and decide to remember that day—whatever may have happened—as a day to be grateful for. In so doing we increase our heart's capacity to choose joy.

HENRI J. M. NOUWEN

The purposes of a person's heart are deep waters,
but one who has insight draws them out.

PROVERBS 20:5 NIV

We are forgiven and righteous because of Christ's sacrifice; therefore
we are pleasing to God in spite of our failures. Christ alone
is the source of our forgiveness, freedom, joy, and purpose.

ROBERT S. MCGEE

Wealth is worthless in the day of wrath, but righteousness delivers from death. The righteousness of the blameless makes their paths straight, but the wicked are brought down by their own wickedness. The righteousness of the upright delivers them, but the unfaithful are trapped by evil desires.

When Jesus was on earth, it wasn't an accident that He came
as a blue-collar worker, nor that His parables would deal with things
like sowing seed, vineyard laborers, harvesters, house building, and swine tending.
In Him there is no hierarchy of importance vocationally,
there's only the wise use of the talents He dispenses.

LARRY KREIDER

Do you see someone skilled in their work? They will serve before kings; they will not serve before officials of low rank.

This voice that calls to us out of the everyday moments of life is called the wisdom of God. This wisdom is infused into nature and the laws that govern her, and into human nature and the laws that govern it.

KEN GIRE

The wicked bluff their way through, but the virtuous think before they act.
No human wisdom or understanding or plan can stand against the LORD.

Have confidence in God's mercy, for when you think
He is a long way from you, He is often quite near.

THOMAS À KEMPIS

People who conceal their sins will not prosper,
but if they confess and turn from them, they will receive mercy.

The less we have, the more we give.
Seems absurd, but it's the logic of love.

MOTHER TERESA

The cheerful of heart has a continual feast. Better is a little with the fear of the LORD than great treasure and trouble with it.

PROVERBS 15:15–16 ESV

What we need is not new light, but new sight; not new paths, but new strength to walk in the old ones; not new duties but new wisdom from on High to fulfill those that are plain before us.

The path of life leads upward for the wise;
they leave the grave behind.

PROVERBS 15:24 NLT

Love is the only force capable
of transforming an enemy into a friend.

MARTIN LUTHER KING JR.

If your enemies are hungry, give them food to eat.
If they are thirsty, give them water to drink. You will heap burning coals...
on their heads, and the Lord will reward you.

If your determination is fixed, I do not counsel you to despair.
Few things are impossible to diligence and skill.
Great works are performed not by strength, but perseverance.

SAMUEL JOHNSON

The soul of the sluggard craves and gets nothing,
while the soul of the diligent is richly supplied.

Neither let mistakes nor wrong directions...discourage you.
There is precious instruction to be got by finding we were wrong.

THOMAS CARLYLE

Listen to advice and accept discipline, and at the end
you will be counted among the wise.

PROVERBS 19:20 NIV

You can trust the Lord too little,
but you can never trust Him too much.

He who heeds the word wisely will find good,
and whoever trusts in the LORD, happy is he.

PROVERBS 16:20 NKJV

I am happy in having learned to distinguish between ownership and possession.
Books, pictures, and all the beauty of the world belong to those who love
and understand them—not usually to those who possess them.
All of these things that I am entitled to I have—I own them by divine right.
So I care not a bit who possesses them.

JAMES HOWARD KEHLER

Honor the LORD with your possessions, and with the firstfruits
of all your increase; so your barns will be filled with plenty,
and your vats will overflow with new wine.

PROVERBS 3:9–10 NKJV

A loving heart is the truest wisdom.

CHARLES DICKENS

The generous will themselves be blessed,
for they share their food with the poor.

PROVERBS 22:9 NIV

In the beginning, as we are learning to pray, our will is in a struggle with God's will. In time, however, we begin to enter into a grace-filled releasing of our will and a flowing into the will of the Father.

RICHARD J. FOSTER

First, help me never to tell a lie. Second, give me neither poverty nor riches!
Give me just enough to satisfy my needs.

PROVERBS 30:8 NLT

There is no more liberating experience than the joy of loving one's spouse and children, the confidence of being loved, and the knowledge that such love can move mountains and make nations whole.

GARY BAUER

The father of godly children has cause for joy. What a pleasure
to have children who are wise. So give your father and mother joy!
May she who gave you birth be happy.

People who deal with life generously and large-heartedly
go on multiplying relationships to the end.

ARTHUR CHRISTOPHER BENSON

A generous person will prosper;
whoever refreshes others will be refreshed.

PROVERBS 11:25 NIV

With God our trust can be abandoned, utterly free. In Him are no limitations, no flaws, no weaknesses. His judgment is perfect, His knowledge of us is perfect, His love is perfect. God alone is trustworthy.

EUGENIA PRICE

Know also that wisdom is like honey for you: If you find it,
there is a future hope for you, and your hope will not be cut off.

God possesses infinite knowledge and an awareness which is uniquely His.
At all times, even in the midst of any type of suffering, I can realize that He
knows, loves, watches, understands, and more than that, He has a purpose.

BILLY GRAHAM

Many are the plans in a person's heart,
but it is the LORD's purpose that prevails.

PROVERBS 19:21 NIV

Do not take over much thought for tomorrow. God, who has led you safely on so far, will lead you on to the end. Be altogether at rest in the loving holy confidence which you ought to have in His heavenly Providence.

FRANCIS DE SALES

The name of the LORD is a fortified tower:
the righteous run to it and are safe.

PROVERBS 18:10 NIV

If the Lord be with us, we have no cause of fear. His eye is upon us,
His arm over us, His ear open to our prayer—
His grace sufficient, His promise unchangeable.

JOHN NEWTON

The fear of the LORD leads to life,
and whoever has it rests satisfied; he will not be visited by harm.

PROVERBS 19:23 ESV

What steps of wisdom lead us to a place of trust? Let us look for what is good in our situation. Minimize what is bad. Calmly, quietly trust in God. Relax and let God take full control. Yes, quietly trust.

THELMA MCMILLAN